DUNYA MIKHAIL

The Iraqi Nights

الليالي العراقية

- painting from Frankenstein in Baghdad
- critical essay/explanation on One
thousand + one Nights

ALSO BY DUNYA MIKHAIL

The War Works Hard
Diary of a Wave Outside the Sea
Fifteen Iraqi Poets (editor)

DUNYA MIKHAIL

The Iraqi Nights

الليالي العراقية

Translated from the Arabic by Kareem James Abu-Zeid

A NEW DIRECTIONS BOOK

Some of these poems first appeared in *Banipal*, *Epiphany*, *Guernica*, NPR
Books, *Poetry*, *Prairie Schooner*, *Stonecutter*, and *The Texas Observer*.

Manufactured in the United States of America
First published as a New Directions Paperbook (NDP1292) in 2014
Design by Eileen Baumgartner

Library of Congress Cataloging-in-Publication Data
Mikha'il, Dunya, 1965–
[Poems. Selections. English]
The Iraqi nights = al-Layali al-'Iraqiyya / Dunya Mikhail ;
translated from the Arabic by Kareem James Abu-Zeid.
pages cm
ISBN 978-0-8112-2286-0 (alk. paper)
I. Abu-Zeid, Kareem James, translator. II. Title.
PJ7846.I392I3913 2014
892.7'16—dc23   2013050010

10 9 8 7 6 5 4

New Directions Books are published for James Laughlin
by New Directions Publishing Corporation
80 Eighth Avenue, New York 10011
ndbooks.com

CONTENTS

The Iraqi Nights

الليالي العراقية

THE IRAQI NIGHTS

PRELUDE

In the land of Sumer, where the houses are packed so closely together that their walls touch, where people sleep on rooftops in the summer and lovers climb the walls to see one another, and where lovers marry young, though their parents always refuse at first… In that land, Ishtar was walking through the souk looking for a gift for Tammuz. She wanted to buy everything, even the skull hanging there like the ring around the neck of a dove—a dove stepping into what it thinks is the fragment of a setting sun. And the card she forgot to pay for contains neither Cupid nor his arrows, neither fire nor water nor air nor earth; it does not show her bending over the grave, and it does not tell her story on the thousand and second night.

On her way back, she was kidnapped by some masked men. They dragged her onward, leaving her mother's outstretched hand behind her forever. They brought her down into the underworld through seven gates. These poems Ishtar wrote on the gates suggest that she wasn't killed at once. Or perhaps her words drew her abductors' attention away from thoughts of murder.

One Thousand + one Nights, cupid, etc

3

Synecdoche

Her hand holding a gift,
her mother's outstretched hand behind her,
the hand of her childhood doll, who sings when you press a button,
the hand of her abductor, dragging her along,
the hand that wipes away a tear,
the hand that turns over the nights
in an old calendar,
the hand that waves in greeting
or farewell
or for help,
the hand with all its lines:
the line of life,
the line of love,
the line of fate...

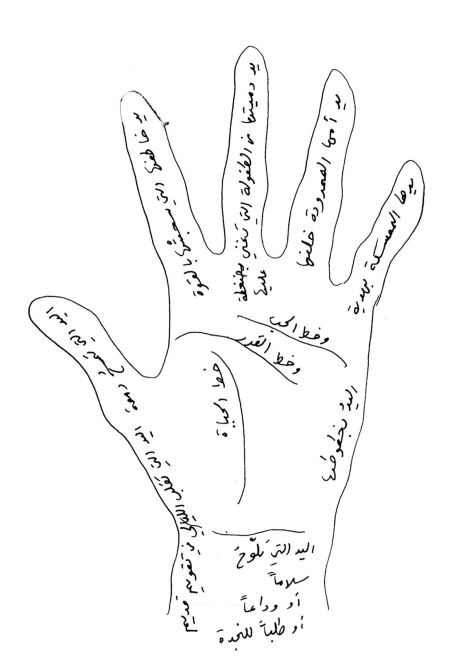

يد أمها المهددة خلفك

يد دميتك أو الطفولة التي تحني بأطفظ عليك

بيدها المسكية بيدك

يد طفل يشير إلى نفسه أو إلى أخيه

يد خاطئة

وخط الحب
وخط القدر
اليد بخطوطك

هذا الخيال

اليد التي تلوّح
سلامة
أو وداعاً
أو طلباً للنجدة

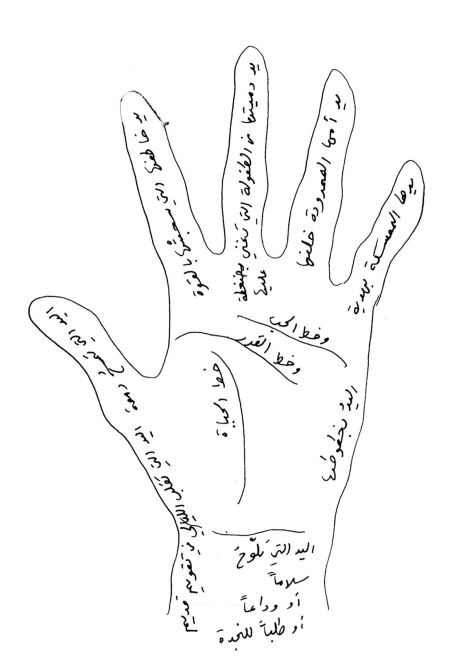

1.
In the first year of war
they played "bride and groom"
and counted everything on their fingers:
their faces reflected in the river;
the waves that swept away their faces
before disappearing;
and the names of newborns.
Then the war grew up
and invented a new game for them:
the winner is the one
who returns from the journey
alone,
full of stories of the dead
as the passing wings flutter
over the broken trees;
and now the winner must tow the hills of dust
so lightly that no one feels it;
and now the winner wears a necklace
with half a metal heart for a pendant,
and the task to follow
is to forget the other half.
The war grew old
and left the old letters,
the calendars and newspapers,
to turn yellow
with the news,
with the numbers,
and with the names
of the players.

[handwritten annotation: personification of war]

[handwritten annotation: body as holding trauma / stories of others, one person as representative of many]

2.
Five centuries have passed
since Scheherazade told her tale.
Baghdad fell,
and they forced me to the underworld.
I watch the shadows
as they pass behind the wall:
none look like Tammuz.
He would cross thousands of miles
for the sake of a single cup of tea
poured by my own hand.
I fear the tea is growing cold:
cold tea is worse than death.

Ishtar?

3.

I would not have found this cracked jar
if it weren't for my loneliness,
which sees gold in all that glitters.
Inside the jar is the magic plant
that Gilgamesh never stopped looking for.
I'll show it to Tammuz when he comes,
and we'll journey, as fast as light,
to all the continents of the world,
and all who smell it will be cured
or freed,
or will know its secret.
I don't want Tammuz to come too late
to hear my urgent song.

4.

When Tammuz comes
I'll also give him all the lists I made
to pass the time:
lists of food,
of books,
lost friends,
favorite songs,
list of cities to see before one dies,
and lists of ordinary things
with notes to prove
that we are still alive.

5.

It's as if I'm hearing music in the boat's hull,
as if I can smell the river, the lily, the fish,
as if I'm touching the skies that fall from the words "I love you,"
as if I can see those tiny notes that are read over and over again,
as if I'm living the lives of birds who bear nothing but their feathers.

6.
The earth circled the sun
once more
and not a cloud
nor wind
nor country
passed through my eyes.
My shadow,
imprisoned in Aladdin's lamp,
mirrors the following:
a picture of the world with you inside,
light passing through a needle's eye,
scrawlings akin to cuneiform,
hidden paths to the sun,
dried clay,
tranquil Ottoman pottery,
and a huge pomegranate, its seeds
scattered all over Uruk.

all contained by the shadow

meaning of the pomegranate?

focus on future repair

7.
In Iraq,
after a thousand and one nights,
someone will talk to someone else.
Markets will open
for regular customers.
Small feet will tickle
the giant feet of the Tigris.
Gulls will spread their wings
and no one will fire at them.
Women will walk the streets
without looking back in fear.
Men will give their real names
without putting their lives at risk.
Children will go to school
and come home again.
Chickens in the villages
won't peck at human flesh   *theme of*
on the grass.   *dismemberment*
Disputes will take place
without any explosives.
A cloud will pass over cars
heading to work as usual.
A hand will wave
to someone leaving
or returning.
The sunrise will be the same
for those who wake
and those who never will.
And every moment   *longing for*
something ordinary   *the ordinary in the*
will happen   *face of a nightmare*
under the sun.

TABLETS

1.

She pressed her ear against the shell:
she wanted to hear everything
he never told her.

2.

A single inch
separates their two bodies
facing one another
in the picture:
a framed smile
buried beneath the rubble.

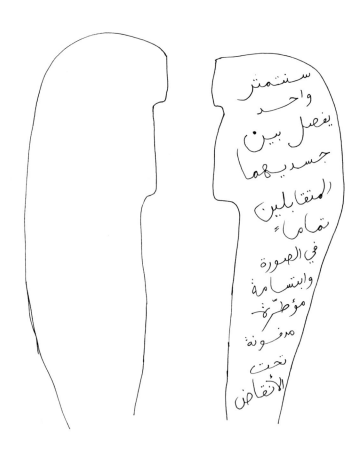

3.
Whenever you throw stones
into the sea
it sends ripples through me.

4.
My heart's quite small:
that's why it fills so quickly.

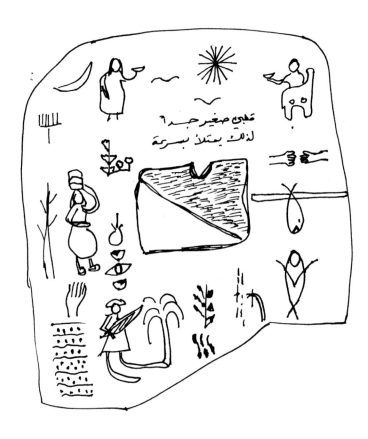

5.
Water needs no wars
to mix with water
and fill the blank spaces.

6.
The tree doesn't ask why it's not moving
to some other forest
nor any other pointless questions.

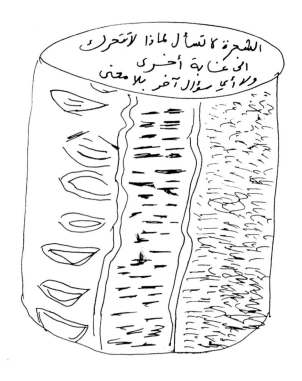

7.
He watches TV
while she holds a novel.
On the novel's cover
there's a man watching TV
and a woman holding a novel.

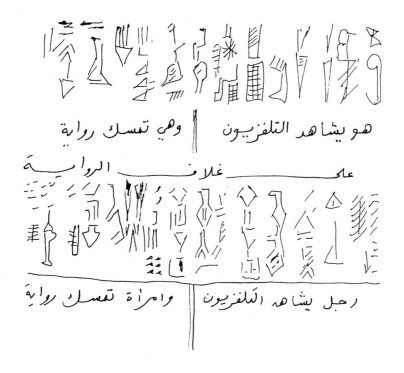

8.

On the first morning
of the new year
all of us will look up
at the same sun.

9.
She raised his head to her chest.
He did not respond:
he was dead.

10.

The person who gazed at me for so long,
and whose gaze I returned for just as long...
That man who never once embraced me,
and whom I never once embraced...
The rain wrecked the colors around him
on that old canvas.

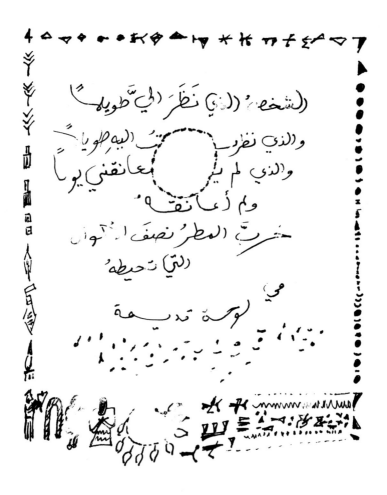

11.
He was not with the husbands
who were lost and then found;
he did not come with the prisoners of war,
nor with the kite that took her,
in her dream,
to some other place,
while she stood before the camera
to have her smile
glued into the passport.  synecdoche

23

12.
Dates piled high
beside the road:
your way
of kissing me.

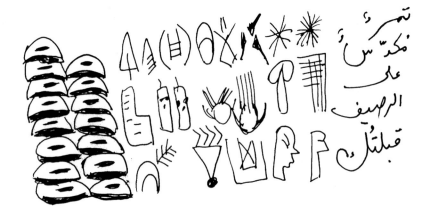

13.
Rapunzel's hair
reaching down
from the window
to the earth
is how we <u>wait</u>.

[handwritten annotation: scheme of waiting connected w/ myth/story]

شَعَر
رابنزل
الممدود
من
النافذة
الى
الأرض،
أنتظاراتنا

14.

The shadows ~~focus on shadows~~
the prisoners left
on the wall
surrounded the jailer
and cast light
on his loneliness.

15.

Homeland, I am not your mother,
so why do you weep in my lap like this
every time
something hurts you?

16.
Never mind this bird:
it comes every day
and stops at the branch's edge
to sing for an hour
or two.
That's all it does:
nothing makes it happier.

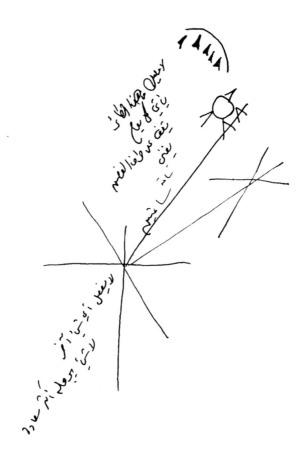

17.
House keys,
identity cards,
faded pictures among the bones...
All of these are scattered
in a single mass grave.

& documents as
relics,
almost
bodily

18.
The Arabic language
loves long sentences
and long wars.
It loves never-ending songs
and late nights
and weeping over ruins.
It loves working
for a long life
and a long death.

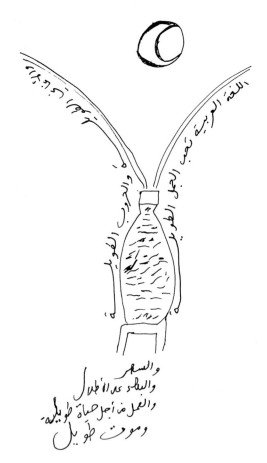

19.
Far away from home—
that's all that changed in us.

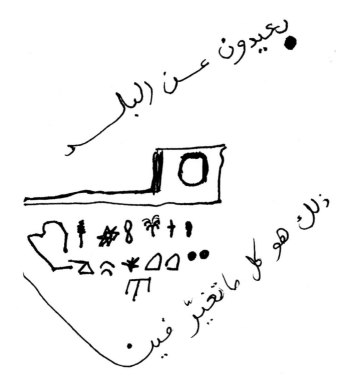

20.
Cinderella left her slipper in Iraq
along with the smell of cardamom
wafting from the teapot,
and that huge flower,
its mouth gaping like death.

21.
Instant messages
ignite revolutions.
They spark new lives
waiting for a country to download,
a land that's little more
than a handful of dust
when faced with these words:
"There are no results that match your search."

رسائل الكترونية سريعة
تشعل ثورات
وحيوات جديدة
في انتظار تحميل وطن,
ليس حفنة تراب
بوجه هذه العبارة :
« لا شيء مطابقة لهذا البحث »

22.
The dog's excitement
as she brings the stick to her owner
is the moment of opening the letter.

23.
We cross borders lightly
like clouds.
Nothing carries us,
but as we move on
we carry rain,
and an accent,
and a memory
of another place.

مثل الغيوم
نعبرُ الحدودَ بخفّة
لاشيءَ يحملنا
لكننا في سيرنا
نحملُ ذاكرةَ
معالمٍ آخرَ
ومطرًا
ولكنة

24.
How thrilling to appear in his eyes.
She can't understand what he's saying:
she's too busy chewing his voice.
She looks at the mouth she'll never kiss,
at the shoulder she'll never cry on,
at the hand she'll never hold,
and at the ground where their shadows meet.

shadows as
sometim
left over /a
memory

كم مثير أن تظهر في عينيه
لاتفهم مايقوله لها
مشغولة بمضغ صوته في فمها
تنظر إلى فمه الذى لن تقبّله
الى كتفه الذى لن تبكى فوقه
الى يده التى لن تلمسها
الى الأرض حيث ظلاهما يلتقيان

THE SHAPE OF THE WORLD

If the world were flat
like a flying carpet,
our sorrow would have a beginning
and an end.

If the world were square,
we'd lie low in a corner
whenever the war
plays hide and seek.

If the world were round,
our dreams would take turns
on the Ferris wheel,
and we'd all be equal.

THE END OF THE WORLD

For Lori, who says "everything is happening now"

Everything is telling me
it's the end of the world:
the astrologers,
the deadly new viruses,
the ozone layer,
the ant cavorting with the grasshopper,
the wars,
and his message, cold and curt.
But other things change my mind:
the clouds that always know their way,
the seashell that hasn't quite disclosed all,
the wishes tossed with coins into the fountain,
and the flower, waiting to happen.

I hope / for u

THREE WOMEN

That stone is three women—
it was cast there ten years ago.
No one touched its pain,
no one heard it wail,
no one saw it dream of the sun.
Feathers scattered everywhere: its memories.
Another night on the way to the cages,
and the stars, dead eggs glistening, don't know
the secret of the stone.
They move slowly above
the neighbors who enter their homes
and turn off the lights.
Another morning will rise
beyond the three shadows
crammed inside the stone.

THE PLANE

The plane arriving from Baghdad
carries American soldiers:
it rises above the moon
reflected on the Tigris,
above clouds piled like corpses,
and an ancient harp,
and the beaten breasts,
and the ones who were kidnapped;
it rises above
the destruction that grows with the children,
and the long lines at the passport office,
and Pandora's open box.
The plane and its exhausted passengers
will land six thousands miles away
from an amputated finger
lying in the sand.

lost / abandoned limbs

AT THE MUSEUM

A small Sumerian goddess
stands behind the glass,
her raised hands
touching the sky.

On my second visit
the goddess has grown:
she's slightly bent over,
her lowered hands
pointing to the earth.

On my third visit
she lays down,
her hands to the side
in preparation for sleep.

On my last visit
she closes her eyes,
her hands across her chest:
is she hiding a secret?

IN THE AQUARIUM

A fish
meets another fish
and lays eggs.
As its fins signal to the seaweed
its colors come out
one after the other.
Its bubbles are words
meant for no one.
The world rises and falls
each day
through the eyes of a fish.

A SECOND LIFE

[handwritten: a new beginning]

After this life
we'll need a second life
to apply what we learned
in the first.

We make one mistake
after another
and need a second life
to forget.

We hum endlessly
as we wait for the departed:
we need a second life
for the whole song.

We go to war
and do everything Simon says:
we need a second life
for love alone.

We need time
to serve out our prison terms
so we can live free
in our second life.

We learn a new language
but need a second life
to practice it.

We write poetry and pass away,
and need a second life
to know the critics' opinions.

We rush around
all over the place
and need a second life
to stop and take pictures.

Suffering takes time:
we need a second life
to learn to live
without pain.

connect second life to Frankenstein's monster? Rebirth as a way to cope w/ or process war?

YOUR E-MAIL

When your name appears on the screen,
all the planets converge for me,
and even Pluto joins in;
the vine ripens for me
and extends to the neighbors' garden;
Ishtar comes back to life
to sing a song
for the wrecked cities;
she washes the dust from her face,
spins, graceful as a dancer,
sends all the soldiers home,
and sets the sparrow's broken leg—
it too was wounded
in the land between two rivers.

Ishtar's leaving through the gate,
but I'm still waiting for your e-mail:
the screen reflects a pair of weary eyes
while the hands of my watch embrace
in the middle of your silence.

45

FORGOTTEN MOON

For Sandra Day O'Connor

He has a long story,
and so does she:
details,
events,
and people.
None of it matters
to their entwined fingers
at this moment
in this place of oblivion.
Eighty years went by:
voices grew distant,
doors were opened
and closed,
places filled up
and emptied out,
while the wind
swept away the names
and the dates
and the notes
and...
All of it dissolved in the river
that flowed behind them.
He has a long story,
and so does she.
He tells her nothing,
and she does the same.
A half-moon rises:
no one knows
where the other half is hiding.

IRAQIS AND OTHER MONSTERS

They are terrifying.
Their heads are dark and tremulous;
they roam the desert
in the form of bulls and lions,
with swords gleaming in their eyes.
They rub their moustaches when they make promises
or threats,
or when they flirt.
Smoke pours out
of their massive noses
and rises to the sky.
They shake the earth with such strength
it wakes the dead.
They live in darkness
without water or electricity.
Dust is their food, clay their bread.
They know neither sleep nor rest.
The war visits them every day
with new baskets of bones.
They have strange customs:
the Sunnis say the Shiites all have tails;
the Shiites carry keys to Heaven in their pockets
in case of sudden death;
the Kurds take to the mountains when they fight
and when they dance the *dabka*;
the Chaldeans consult the stars in all decisions;
the Assyrians put feathers on their heads
to prove they've vanquished the eagle;
the Armenians throw themselves in the river
whenever they're annoyed;
the Mandaeans celebrate their festivals
by staying home for three full days;
the Yezidis honor the Devil

and consecrate lettuce;
the Turkomans are always waiting
for the Sultan to return.
When the sun sets
and the guns fall silent,
these Iraqis and other monsters
take out their ouds
and make music for the missing
together
until morning.

FOOTPRINTS ON THE MOON

When I set foot on the moon
everything told me that you were there, too:
my lighter weight,
the loss of gravity,
my heart's rapid beating,
my mind empty of everyday concerns,
the lack of memories of any kind,
the earth off in another place,
and these footprints...
All of this points to you.

THE GAZE OF ORPHEUS

What if he hadn't killed her
with his gaze?
They'd be in the kitchen now
making coffee
or talking
about the endless war,
or blowing out candles
for their thousandth anniversary,
ghosts dancing all around them;
or they'd be listening to a song
whose name they've forgotten;
or coughing amid a million specks of flying dust;
or sitting together, simply,
like two statues of salt.

dust /rubble/
debris as a
consistent theme

THE OLD OLIVE TREE

The city changed
and the scene beyond the smoke
gradually became clearer.
Holes everywhere:
in the walls of houses,
and the walls of the heart,
and the tail of a cat.
An empty suitcase
open
to the horizon.
Arabs and Israelis
exchanging glances:

—I'm Joseph,
and these are my brothers,
and this is her knife,
and the well is deep,
as deep as my wound,
so why have you raised a house
on top of my grave?

—Where should I raise it, then?
The land closed in on me
and drove me away.
I wandered for ages
until I arrived
back where I started,
so I sat down here
like an exclamation point.

—I left that same spot
and to it

51

I return.
I return
like the seasons and the rain
even if it's all
out of order.

—This is the seed I planted
in this land
where you found me:
I was banished
before my fruit ripened.

—You've got your story
and I've got mine:
two different beginnings
but the end is the same.

—And between the beginning
and the end
are all those details
that are killing you
and killing me.

—And because the plot was hard to follow,
it bored the readers:
they fell asleep
and saw us as nightmares,
and that was the end of it.

—So let's cast our stories into the sea
and move on.

—Tomorrow,
when your grandchildren and mine
are playing around the old olive tree,

they'll find dried blood on its trunk
and see how we scratched our alphabets,
Arabic and Hebrew,
into it
until it turned red
and its leaves dried up
and fell on the bodies.

—And when they grow up
they'll sit in its shade
and, as if in Plato's cave, guess
the meanings of our shadows
scattered
there
behind the old olive tree.

A DEBATE

"The moon is our neighbor,"
sings Fairouz,
while the taxi driver adjusts the mirror
but still misses some images:
a sheer scarf on a bench,
empty bottles scattered around,
coffee grinds on the rooftops,
tattered flags,
abandoned pomegranate seeds
(what seeds fell from heaven?),
and a debate:

—This is my land,
and if you don't believe me, ask the seasons,
for they know how to leave
and how to return.

—No, this is my land,
and if you don't believe me, ask the birds,
for they know the way home.

—Let's go ask the ruler of the land,
so that we may know the truth.

—Let's go to the rain, then.

—Raindrop, you with your great wisdom always know the way to the
earth. So tell us: Who owns this land?

And the raindrop replied: I mix with the other raindrops and give
no thought to what land I'm falling on. The cloud is the one who
sends me. Ask the cloud.

—Cloud, you with your great wisdom always know your way in the sky, and how to send the rain to the earth. Tell us: Who owns this land?

And the cloud replied: I pass by with the other clouds and give no thought to what land I'm floating above. The wind is the one who sends me. Ask the wind.

—Wind, you with your great wisdom know every direction, and you are the one who propels the clouds. Tell us: Who owns this land?

And the wind replied: I move through the whole world, and the tree responds but never follows me. Ask the tree.

—Tree, you with your great wisdom extend your roots into the earth and greet the world with your branches. Tell us: Who owns this land?

And the tree replied: My roots are happy within, and my branches are happy without. The seed is my teacher. Ask the seed.

But the seed was busy feeding the land and had no time to answer.

TEARS

I work in a store that sells tears
in bottles of all shapes and sizes—
a crowded place
with no time for handkerchiefs.
First in line is that woman
who comes in every day
to buy these colorless drops.
Are they for her, or for others?
Next, a new customer:
he once thought he'd never leave his country,
not even if the mountains themselves
were torn from the ground.
Next comes a boy with his grandmother:
they survived the Flood—
well, not exactly.
The woman at the end of the line
wants to return her bottle:
she says she did not open it;
she had thought she would need it
after her friend left her,
but instead she just went back
and forth
between two parking spots.
The sun has left for the world's other half.
Time to go home:
we are all out of tears.

SONG FROM ANOTHER TIME

A song from another time
survived with me.
It follows me wherever I go.
It rushes after me.
I crumple it up,
a small piece of paper,
and throw it away.

But I peel the paper open
and smooth it out
whenever I remember
one of my dead friends.

[handwritten annotation: rhizomatic time / sense of accumulation]

AN EARTHQUAKE

For the people of Haiti

In the first minute
a branch shook
beneath the bird's talons.
In the second minute
the whole city shook
beneath the bird.
The bird could not grasp
the extreme speed
of the fall:
the boy bathing in the river,
the drowned man behind him,
the tourist in the white boat,
the student slipping a note for a rendezvous
into her pocket,
the shared taxi
that ran out of gas,
the mother yelling at her son
because he was in the street instead of at school,
the singer with the *tambu* drum,
the naked dancers beneath the sun,
and the little girl with her broken doll:
in a single minute
they plunged into the earth,
and all the trees beneath the birds
fell away—
this time
not for the sake of paper,
or the white boat,
or the note slipped into the pocket,
or for the school
or for the gas,

or the houses or the drum,
and not for the sake of the little girl
or her doll.

Is   this   a sign   then?
This page   floating   in the   air?
This   floating page   from   a   half-burned   book?
This   half-burned   book   on   al-Mutanabbi   Street?
Al-Mutanabbi Street,   whose tales were cut short by a bomb?
That bomb   that scattered   all   those pages?
As if   searching   desperately   for some meaning?
This very page   from   *The Ring of the Dove?*
The one   that flew up   and fell   to the ground again?
The one   that crept in   among   the scattered bodies?
The one   now clinging   to her chest?
Aren't   these   the very same lines?
The ones   that were once   recited   to her?
"As   I   come to you,   I   hurry
like   the full moon   crossing   the sky,
and   as I leave   —if I leave—   I move
as slowly   as the stars   fixed in the sky."

PERSONAL HISTORY

1. THE STORY

The story I wished to whisper in your ears
was condensed in the cup
on the table
as I waited for Flight 65,
and then it was coiled in the gate
through which the passengers entered
hastily
and indifferently.
The story I wished to whisper
was curled up
in the stamp
in the passport.
The story I wished for...
appeared on the buildings
through the car window
and was moving
in the other direction.
The story turned
with the key
and entered the apartment
alone.

2. THE IMAGE

In a moment of boredom
I turn the album's pages
and stop at a picture
where we're all smiling
in a place I no longer know.
I can easily translate
the silence of that image
into each and every language.
But I wonder:
What made you leave your other image
back there in the mirror?

3. THE FLOWER

I stretched my hands out
like branches,
pressed my feet
into the earth,
while ideas whorled
around my head.
I bent, waiting
to be plucked
or at least smelled.
But the flower was the flower:
it was not me.

CHINA

1. AN OIL PAINTING IN BEIJING

I see serpents coiling
around the neck of a woman
I do not know.
Beside her,
ashen mountains.
In front, a dog
who is said to be
the New Year.
Behind, two men
bargaining.
An inch farther,
slender figures
intertwined
from the earth
to the sky.

2. LIU XIAOBO

All those stars that fell
on the prison roof
would still not fill
your empty seat.

HONG KONG

1. THE BIG BUDDHA

Flowers
everywhere:
on porcelain
and bracelets
and ashtrays,
on silk ties
and coat hems,
on carpets
and walls,
in meals
and speech,
in paintings
and on teacups.
Flowers that smell like fish,
flowers blooming in the mouths,
in people's shy laughter,
flowers glistening in their eyes,
flowers swaying in her hands:
flowers piled up for Buddha
as he sits, a lotus
pointing the way.

2. IN THE FISHERMEN'S VILLAGE

Through windows without glass
the houses spill water
and fish
and legends
into the river.
The fishermen gaze at us,
newcomers from a skyscraper
in Hong Kong.
We gaze at them
from a boat
that moves through their waters
without their permission.
They gaze at us, passing clouds,
from ramshackle homes,
and we gaze back
at the old tin sheets.
We watch
their watery lives
across the river.
They watch
our arid lives
that cross the river.

SMOOTH ROCK

For Kazuko Shiraishi

Your heart a smooth rock,
you forget it
on the table
and leave happily
as if following a bird
that carries the secret in its beak.
You stop
to unfurl the giant piece of paper
from your heart
to your feet:
your Japanese characters
are cities
of eggs
falling
before
our eyes.

FLAWCHART

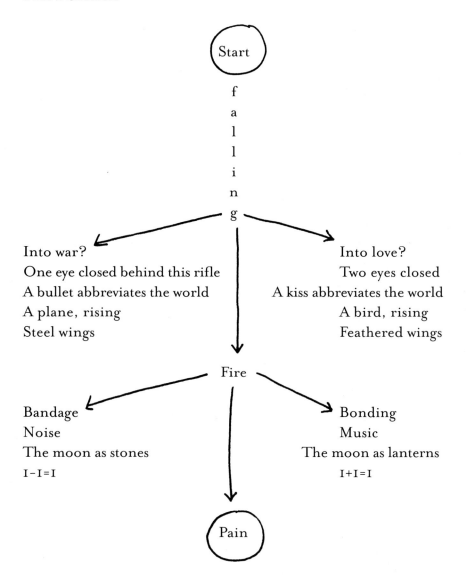

Start

f
a
l
l
i
n
g

Into war?   Into love?
One eye closed behind this rifle   Two eyes closed
A bullet abbreviates the world   A kiss abbreviates the world
A plane, rising   A bird, rising
Steel wings   Feathered wings

Fire

Bandage   Bonding
Noise   Music
The moon as stones   The moon as lanterns
$I-I=I$ $I+I=I$

Pain

ANOTHER PLANET

I have a special ticket
to another planet
beyond this Earth.
A comfortable world, and beautiful:
a world without much smoke,
not too hot
and not too cold.
The creatures
are gentler there,
and the governments
have no secrets.
The police are nonexistent:
there are no problems
and no fights.
And the schools
don't exhaust their students
with too much work
for history has yet to start
and there's no geography
and no other languages.
And even better:
the war
has left its "r" behind
and turned into love,
so the weapons sleep
beneath the dust,
and the planes pass by
without shelling the cities,
and the boats
look like smiles
on the water.
All things

are peaceful
and kind
on the other planet
beyond this Earth.
But still I hesitate
to go alone.

*loneliness, fellow
feelings, etc*

THE SOLD PARROT

Everything is new
today
for the parrot:
Where's the silver fish
that used to greet the parrot with its tail,
the bubbles flowing from its mouth?
Where's the tank with all its stars?
Where's the little boy
who always stopped
to stare at it
and sometimes even tried to touch it?
And most importantly of all:
where's the woman who used to feed it from her hand
while he repeated after her:
habibi—"beloved."
Habibi?

MURMURS AT THE INTENSIVE CARE UNIT

—He was in the coffee shop when he fainted.
—No, he's never suffered a heart attack before.
—He has a life he must return to.
—He can't just leave like that without a word.
—He loves photography and the smell of coffee.
—What does it mean when the machine beeps?
—Did you see the last picture he sent?
—He's scared of injections.
—He was planning a trip to Michigan.
—He's breathing through the machine.
—There's hope if he'd only open his eyes.
—But he moved his hand a little when she spoke.
—His voice mail is full.

CHOICES

"Paper or plastic?"
I'm not sure how to respond.
I wish I'd had such a choice
in more pressing matters
long ago
when I was in a country
that cared less
about our choices
or what kind of bags we used.

DREAMS

1.
Yesterday I dreamt of you:
I was drowning
and you saved me
then gave me a long kiss.
When I woke
I was sorry:
I won't have the chance
anytime soon
to drown again.

2.

I dreamt I fell into a hole
and when I woke
I found a feather.
If only I'd put it under my pillow
before going to sleep:
I'd have dreamt I was a dove
and wouldn't have fallen.

THE DROWNED MAN

It's as if she's starting to believe
with each passing day
that he's no longer in this world.
Ever since they brought her his hat
and the news
that he had drowned in the sea
she's been going out to sit in front of the house
then quickly coming in again
as if she'd forgotten something.
She puts the mail where it belongs.
She reads his horoscope in the papers.
She feeds his bird in the corner.
She rushes to the phone each time it rings.
She looks at the house's sole tree
as it suddenly changes colors:
the new season has arrived like a prisoner
emerging into the street's blinding light
for the very first time.
She rubs her eyes,
puts his picture back in her purse,
and weeps.
It's as if she's starting to believe it.

OTHER PRONOUNS

You study history,
I study your eyes:
we make the world go round.

You become a dot in the distance,
I become a dot in the distance:
we see a line between the dots.

You come closer,
I come closer:
we rise like lunar dough.

You bring the box of war games,
I open it:
we release broken wooden figures.

RETURNING

The bird flies into its nest
with more straw.
Leaves shattering in the forest,
hasty footsteps beneath the rain.
I do not want wings,
only his plume,
my lover's plume.

...

The snows covered me
a thousand years ago
and I've been sleeping ever since.
I do not want the sun,
only his kiss,
my lover's kiss.

...

He must be a moon
that I see him everywhere.
I don't turn to gold when touched
but I shine
like a distant star.

...

Floods appeared

and disappeared,
and gypsies came
and went
while I sang him morning and night:
perhaps he'll rise,
rise with my voice,
perhaps my lover will rise with my voice.

...

The soldiers
returned home
and the hats
returned to people's heads.

...

The leaves
dried up,
then turned green again,
then yellow,
then shattered
in the forest,
and the bird returned
with more straw.

LARSA

As if the world's last egg
were about to fall from me
onto the ground:
that's how I move
with you inside me.

As if you were drawing shapes
on the way to growing up:
the circle's a woman who swallowed the globe;
the rectangle a moving bed;
the triangle the doctor's face;
the square a clock
heedless of appointments.

As if you were a new prophet
lisping and sending signs to all creation
so that I forget my enemies:
they melt together like gentle snow.

I write your name with chalk
mixing the sun letters
with the moon letters:
Lullabies at night to bring good news; questions
About the exodus and what came after; visions
Revealing the simple pleasure of paper boats; the secret
Spot where we stowed the umbilical cord;
And answers from the rattle.

We divide the world
into bread
or rain
or a coat too big for us,
and we're confused because

—although we shake our wings—
we do not fly.

You yawn,
so I harvest stars from your sleep
and stick them in your notebook:
may they bring you joy
when I'm not here.

You start walking
and follow the moon
while I follow you.
Behind us: the mirage of a country
you were not born in.

You wave your hand
and I know
you're mixing rivers
and lakes
and continents
with a teaspoon or a straw.
You bear the Euphrates and Atlantic, together,
to school.
You spray colors,
dark and light,
at temperatures,
high and low,
and all sides make peace
because you, Larsa, are beautiful.
And like snowballs rolling to a halt,
the countries, for a moment, stop fighting
because you, Larsa,
are beautiful.

You open your arms
and I know just how much I love you:
I love you from here to Baghdad;
I love you more than all the words;
I love you higher
than the smoke in the city;
I love you louder
than the explosions;
I love you deeper than the wounds,
Iraqi and American,
from an IED;
I love you sweeter than a lily
unfolding in the morning;
I love you warmer than a nest
that lacks only birdsong
and a single piece of straw;
I love you wider than the fear
that brims in a time of war;
coming and going
from here to Baghdad
I love you.

enduring nature of maturity?

ABOUT THE AUTHOR

Dunya Mikhail was born in Iraq in 1965. While working as a journal-
ist, she faced increasing threats from the Iraqi authorities and fled
first to Jordan, then to the United States. In 2001, she was awarded
the UN Human Rights Award for Freedom of Writing and in 2013
a Kresge Artist Fellowship. Her first book of poems in English, *The
War Works Hard*, was named one of the twenty-five books to remember
by the New York Public Library in 2005. Her second collection,
Diary of a Wave Outside the Sea, won the 2010 Arab American Book Award
for poetry. She currently lives in Michigan and works as an Arabic
instructor for Oakland University.

Author photograph by Michael Smith